Amazing Animal Adventures

On Islands

with Brian Keating

1

Murrelets on
Haida Gwaii

Vampire Finches and
Firework Oceans

Pahoehoe and AA

Keas and
in Kiwi L

Greenland

Arctic Ocean

Canada

North America

United States

Queen
Charlotte
Islands:
Murrelets on
Haida Gwaii

Europe

Atlantic Ocean

Afri

Hawaii:
Pahoehoe
and AA

Equator

Galapagos Islands:
Vampire Finches and
Firework Oceans

South
America

Malawi:
The Crazy
Cichlids of
Lake Malawi

Pacific Ocean

Southern
Ocean

Searching for the
"Man of the Forest"

The Singing Lemurs
of the Cloud Forest

The

BRIAN KEATING'S AMAZING ANIMAL ADVENTURES

TABLE OF CONTENTS

Asia

Indian Ocean

Pacific Ocean

Sarawak, Borneo:
Searching for the
"Man of the Forest"

Sabah, Borneo:
The Land of
the Hornbill

...agascar:
...Singing
...urs of the
...ud Forest

Papua New Guinea:
Dancing in the Lek with
Birds of Paradise

Australia

New Zealand:
Keas and Kakas
in Kiwi Land

...ntarctic Continent

N

0   1500   3000 km

Keep exploring!

Brian Keating

Dancing in the Lek
with Birds of
Paradise

The Crazy Cichlids
of Lake Malawi

A NATURALIST IS BORN

The first time I was attracted to the magic of islands was when I was a kid, addicted to the TV show *Gilligan's Island*. I watched every episode. And I imagined living on an island like Gilligan's in a bamboo house, sleeping on a bamboo bed, and using all the goofy life-support systems they had. I was really taken by the sound of the kookaburra on that show. That koo-koo-koo-koo-ki-ki-ki-ki-ki-KA-KA-KA sound was always there in the background. It wasn't until I took my first trip to Australia that I realized kookaburras aren't island birds, they're continental Australian birds! I guess the TV producers on *Gilligan's Island* must have thought they sounded exotic.

Islands are exotic and exciting, but they are also places of refuge in a busy world. I suppose that's why the Calgary Zoo has always appealed to me. It's on an island in the middle of a busy city, in the middle of the clean, clear, glacial-fed Bow River. Walking over the bridge that connects the city to the island makes visitors feel that they can cast off their busy lives and relax amongst the world's incredible wildlife.

I have always loved islands, and now I work on one!

Ever since I was a little kid, I liked climbing things. On my first sailing trip to the Queen Charlotte Islands, I spent a lot of time high up on the mast, looking for whales. It was exhilarating.

I also live right across from an island. It is only 25 meters (82 ft.) from my backyard, also in the Bow River. I paddle over to it often and make sure that beavers aren't chopping down too many willows. I clean up garbage that collects on it and watch the birds. I watch red-winged blackbirds singing their little hearts out. Every spring there is an eastern kingbird that comes and nests on the island, and before the spring runoff floods the island, there are always half a dozen Canada geese nesting there. Occasionally I've even seen mink.

In this busy world, I'm sure you long for an island refuge of your own. Islands truly are places of wonder. As you will read in the following pages, they are also ideal places for studying the

Your Own Backyard Adventure
Creating Your Own Natural History Museum

When I was in school, I used to collect items from nature. I once found the skeleton of a dead rat under a barn, and I decided to put it back together. A curator from New York's Museum of Natural History helped me to do that. I still have that skeleton on display in my house! Natural history museums are amazing places that display the workings of nature so people can understand the world better. You and a group of friends can create your own natural history museum, too, one that reflects what is going on in your own backyard.

You will need:
- a large, cardboard box that a television or large appliance came in
- a table
- scissors
- markers or paint
- small cardboard boxes for individual displays
- cue cards for exhibit descriptions
- objects from nature!

The natural objects:
You can find fascinating objects in your own backyard for your museum. Remember to respect your environment as you collect—don't collect living things or objects in use by living things. But, do collect fossils from a nearby river or stream; owl pellets from a stand of trees where an owl family is living; interesting rocks, bones, and feathers; abandoned wasp or bird nests. The list could go on and on. You may even wish to create a museum with a theme: geology, perhaps, if you are interested in rocks.

If you've found something that can be taken apart, take it apart for your exhibit to show what's inside or how it works. Find out as much as you can about the objects. Use cue cards to write out interesting facts about the objects you choose to exhibit.

How to make the exhibit area:
- Cut the large cardboard box so that it folds out and can be set up on a table.
- With markers or paint, decorate the walls of the box with the name of your museum, what the exhibit is about, and where the objects came from. Don't forget to write your names as the "curators" of the museum.
- Decorate the smaller cardboard boxes and place the natural objects in them.

Tours:
- Invite your parents, siblings, and friends to tour your museum.
- Prepare a speech about your museum, featuring your favorite object.
- Because the museum is in a big box, you could also bring your museum to school to show and tell.

way animals and plants evolve. Find out about the amazing animals that manage to survive on some difficult islands, what is threatening their survival, and what people can do to conserve island animals and their environments. I'm always inspired by islands and island creatures. After you read this book, I hope you will be, too.

VAMPIRE FINCHES AND FIREWORK OCEANS

Of all the islands that I've been to, the Galapagos Islands are the most famous. Charles Darwin visited these islands almost 200 years ago and made them famous when he wrote a book called *The Origin of Species*. To explain his theory of evolution, he wrote about how the 13 species of finches on the Galapagos Islands had evolved. Charles Darwin changed the way people would think about life on Earth, forever, by describing the finches' speciation.

It's funny, but Darwin didn't really think about the finches as the keys to his theory until he got back to England. That's when— PING—something went off in his brain. Darwin suddenly realized there might be something amazing about the finches. He was right.

The finches were blown onto the Galapagos Islands about a millennium ago. And they didn't start out as 13 distinct species. They radiated, or evolved, into the species we see today from one single species. Each of the new species adapted to a different source of food on the islands. We can tell them apart by the shapes of their beaks. Their secret to living on the harsh and remote Galapagos Islands is all about beak and behavior adaptation.

We were fortunate to see many Galapagos sea lions—on the beaches and in the ocean. Once I was scuba diving and I felt a tug on my fin. When I turned around to see what it was, it was a mischievous sea lion, smirking at me! He rocketed past me, did some pirouettes in the water, stopped and looked back, then zapped away in no time!

Some of the finches are adapted to eat thick seeds, some for thin seeds. Some beaks are extra long and used for gathering pollen out of cactus flowers. There are no woodpeckers on the Galapagos Islands, so one of the finches has adapted in a behavioral way. I watched this finch actually pick up sharp sticks or spines from cactus plants and poke insects out of plants!

There's another finch called the vampire finch, which I find the most fascinating of them all. It has a beak that's designed for pinching the skin of squabs (baby frigates and baby blue-footed boobies). This feathered vampire pinches the chicks' skin and then laps up the droplets of blood that ooze from the cuts.

SAY THE WORD!

Adaptation: the process by which an organism becomes suited to its environment

Evolution: the process by which organisms come into being through changes in earlier forms of that organism over the course of time

Species: a group of organisms that can interbreed in nature to produce offspring that can reproduce

There is a species of finch that hops all over iguanas. The bird is actually helping the big lizard by eating parasites and skin flakes.

Land iguanas are vegetarians. They eat fruit and pads of *Opuntia* cactus. They often sit beneath these cacti, waiting for the pads to fall off.

But the finches are just one part of the Galapagos story. These special islands also have some wonderful tortoises. The Galapagos Islands are actually named for their tortoises. *Galapagos* means "saddle" in Spanish, referring to the shape of the tortoise's shell.

These great tortoises died out on the mainland of South America thousands of years ago.

Somehow, though, one or two, or maybe more, tortoises made their way to the islands.

How did the tortoises journey to the islands? Maybe the story went like this: A storm carried a pregnant female tortoise away

Male frigate birds are black with a red sac at their throat, called a gular sac. To attract females, males force air into the sac, and it inflates into a fantastic red balloon.

The tortoises wander up to the higher levels at certain times of the year. They tank up with water, then they go back down into the lowlands, where the temperature is warm and the sand is perfect for incubating their eggs.

Not only do Galapagos tortoises migrate on the islands they live on, but they also somehow float from one island to the next. Each tortoise on each island has adapted to its terrain. Slowly, from perhaps only one mother tortoise, about 15 subspecies came to be. Just 11 of those subspecies still exist. This is partly because of people and partly because of the animals that people have introduced to the islands—animals like goats, rats, cats, and dogs.

Introduced species have done a lot of harm on the Galapagos Islands. Goats have stripped islands of their plants, leaving tortoises with nothing to eat. Rats eat tortoise eggs. And dogs and cats eat young tortoises.

In 1835, when Darwin landed on the islands, there were about 250,000 tortoises. By the time from the mainland. She floated like a cork over the incredible distance from the shores of South America to the Galapagos Islands. That tortoise then climbed onto the shores of a Galapagos beach and laid her eggs. The eggs hatched, and the population of Galapagos tortoises began. So now, in a sense, the islands are a sort of life raft for the species!

To survive on the islands isn't easy. But the tortoises have adapted. They can take on and store huge amounts of water. This is a pretty important characteristic on the desert-like Galapagos Islands. The tortoises are also only found on the bigger islands that have hills. This means they can migrate to higher elevations, where it rains more often.

Nocturnal Gulls and Fireworks in the Ocean

The Galapagos Islands have one of two gulls in the world that are active at night. This nocturnal bird is called the swallow-tailed gull. Swallow-tailed gulls hunt squid and other small fish species that are right on the surface of the water. As these fish move around on the surface, they stir up the water. This causes tiny zooplankton species to glow, like fireflies, making little fireworks in the ocean. The fireworks going off left, right, and center make the small fish on the surface visible to the gulls. That's how the gulls capture their prey. I've never seen anything else like it!

We often saw swallow-tailed gulls during the day, nesting on the islands.

8

a conservation center called the Charles Darwin Research Center was opened in 1959, there were only 5,000 tortoises left. This research center tries to keep the islands healthy. The people who work there have put together different programs to help tortoises, and other Galapagos species,

The lava heron is unique to the Galapagos Islands. Its dark gray color allows it to blend in with the lava around it.

Tortoises, like this one at the Darwin Research Station, are perfectly adapted to their surroundings on the islands.

When I went to the islands, I found out how strict the rules are. You have to go with a guide. You have to stay on the trails. You're not allowed to touch any of the animals. The islands are fragile areas that need to be respected. They are perhaps one of the most unique places on Earth, so it's very important that everyone follows the rules.

stay alive and even thrive on the islands.

The center does all kinds of things to help the islands' animals and birds. It has a captive breeding program. This means that people at the center capture tortoises and breed them. Then they keep the babies at the center until they're big enough to avoid wild dogs. Because of this program, there are now about 15,000 tortoises on the islands. The center also aims to get rid of some of the introduced species. The goats are the worst because they eat everything.

BRIAN'S NOTES

Some Galapagos tortoises have shells that are saddle-backed. This kind of shell allows the tortoises to reach high up on cactus plants so they can eat the cactus flowers.

PAHOEHOE AND AA

The first island that I ever explored was Hawaii. In fact, visiting Hawaii was part of my first big trip. My wife, Dee, and I saved our money and we set out for 4 months of adventure. Hawaii was our first stop. Then we went to New Zealand, New Guinea, and Australia. We were keen on exploring islands.

I was interested in islands because of the unique wildlife you find on them. I was especially curious about the endemic, or native, species that you come across on islands. We were told that if we wanted to see the best variety of birds, the island of Kauai was the place to go. So off we went.

Kauai is one of the least populated of all 8 of the Hawaiian Islands, and it still has a big "green" backyard. Its forest habitat is virtually untouched. I guess that's why people call it the "green island." Kauai's Nepali coast has a magnificent trail that's on the side of a cliff. The trail winds in and around the steep volcanic ridges of the island.

While hiking we saw many animals, both endemic and introduced. We saw and held little Hawaiian lizards called Hawaiian skinks. A feral

While we were camping at the Alakai Swamp, a hurricane swept through the Hawaiian Islands. We found a variety of sea creatures washed up on the beach after the storm had passed.

cat, or a wild house cat, stole my freeze-dried pork chop dinner on the first night we camped out! We also saw a wild goat when we were hiking along a very steep part of the trail.

When Captain Cook sailed through the Hawaiian Islands in 1776, he introduced goats and pigs to the islands for his men to collect and eat on return trips. Of course, now we know that when you introduce a species that has no enemies and hasn't co-evolved with the local life forms, there is bound to be trouble. The pigs churned up the forest floor and ate everything they could get their snouts on at ground level, including birds. The goats ate the same sorts of things, just a little bit higher off the ground. And the cats climbed trees, making the lives of birds pretty difficult. As on most islands, there is a real effort in Hawaii to get rid of these introduced species that have made such a mess.

Dee and I were also excited to find out about the birds that live on Hawaii. We drew many birds in our journals and wrote down their key features: the shape of the beak, the color on the face, whether or not there was a patch of white on the throat or on the eye.

These kinds of illustrations are called field notes. Whenever we had a chance, we would find a library and crack open a bird book to find out what we'd seen.

> The first time I saw a skink was on Hawaii. They are amazing lizards and serious insect predators.

One of the birds we wanted to see was the honeycreeper. Honeycreepers have evolved and exploded into a variety of species. Honeycreepers are usually small and fill the same biological niche that hummingbirds fill in North America. They eat nectar, and like bees, they're pollinators. Honeycreepers have long, downward-curved bills that are different lengths and shapes for the different flowers where they seek their nectar.

To find these amazing honeycreepers, Dee and I hiked for a day through mud

BRIAN'S NOTES

The Hawaiian petrel nests in the cracks around the caldera of Mauna Loa and other tall Hawaiian volcanoes. The nesting season is very long, which prepares the chicks for their first flight: a 4,267-meter (14,000-ft.) vertical descent to the ocean. Can you imagine?

As we hiked, we learned about "Pahoehoe" (pronounced pah-hoy-hoy) and "AA." (pronounced ah-ah). Pahoehoe lava is ropey, smooth lava that you can walk on with your bare feet. AA lava is rough and textured—it hurts your feet and makes you say "Ah, Ah!" when you walk on it.

up to our knees! We were determined. The best place to see these birds was a place called the Alakai Swamp on Kauai. This swamp is the wettest place on the planet. It gets about 1,524 cm (600 in.) of rain a year. On the Alakai Swamp trail we came across a few species of honey-creeper: the amakihi, the iwi, and the apapane.

The longest trek we did in Hawaii was a climb to the top of the volcano Mauna Loa on the Big Island of Hawaii. We walked for about a day and a half along hardened lava to reach the top. Hiking on lava is like walking up a long, sloping driveway.

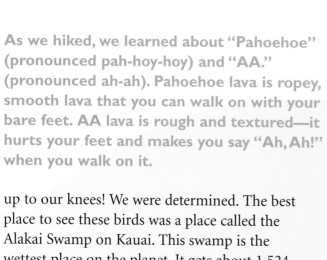

Even fresh lava flows on Mauna Loa had delicate little ferns and fascinating plants called silver swords that grew out of the flows.

The sunrise over Mauna Loa was a beautiful sight. When you are sitting at 4,023 m (13,200 ft.), the sun is much more intense. So we had to apply lots of sunscreen and wore bandanas over our noses and mouths.

While hiking Mauna Loa, we entered this lava tube. It reached far into the side of the volcano, and its walls, ceiling, and floor showed how the lava flowed from the mountain-side.

Walking along, we found long lava tubes where the lava had flowed out of the mountain for a period of time. These rivers of lava develop a skin of dry lava on top of them. When the volcano stops erupting, the remaining liquid lava flows right out of the hardened lava tube, like liquid through a straw, leaving the hardened tube behind. Today, you can walk into these tubes and explore them. Sometimes they're hundreds of meters long.

Finally, we reached the summit cabin at 4,023 meters (13,200 ft.). There was actually snow at the peak! The next day we hiked to Mauna Loa's caldera.

The caldera is the mouth of the volcano where the lava once flowed out. The highest lip of the caldera is the volcano's real summit. When we reached it, we could look down, way down, into the pit of Mauna Loa. There were cracks in the hardened lava below with steam wisping out. It gave us a very real idea of how young and active Mauna Loa still is.

Lava destroys, but it also creates. It builds land that is rich in minerals. There are kinds of plants called pioneer species that are adapted to eke out a living on this new land. These plants begin developing soil that eventually becomes the lush forest that you find on other islands of the Hawaiian chain.

If it weren't for the volcanoes, the Hawaiian Islands wouldn't be there. What an introduction to islands it was for Dee and me, to explore the slopes of volcanoes, the swamps, and the cliff-edge trails of Hawaii's island chain. We jetted off to New Zealand next, hoping for more island adventures.

KEAS AND KAKAS IN KIWI LAND

When Dee and I traveled to New Zealand during our South Pacific islands tour, we hitchhiked everywhere we went. A nun once picked us up and brought us back to her church, where we stayed for the night. A couple of farmers also picked us up, so we ended up on a sheep farm. In New Zealand, people seem to trust everybody.

New Zealand is a remote set of islands, like Hawaii, where there are endemic and unique birds. Dee and I bought a bird book and started organizing gear for a series of treks. We went over mountain passes, up a volcano, and to a remote island called Kapiti.

Kapiti Island is a place that you usually have to apply to visit. Only about 50 people are allowed on it a day because it's a sensitive area. There's usually a 5-month waiting list to visit the place! Dee and I thought we'd give it a try, though, and we went right to the chief ranger. We said, "We're from Canada. We're both biologists and are keenly interested in birds. We're not ordinary tourists." (At least that's how we liked to think of ourselves!) We were lucky. The ranger allowed us to go to Kapiti the next day.

We boarded a small boat and rode across from the main island to Kapiti. We had been hiking all morning, and when we sat down to have lunch, all of a sudden the kakas showed up. The kaka is a type of parrot. They were hanging around to see if there was a free lunch for them!

On Kapiti, we also came across the New Zealand robin, also called a toutouwai.

A kea, inspecting our camera, on a mountain slope. Given the opportunity, I'm sure this inquisitive alpine parrot would have flown away with it!

We found this little bird hopping around on the forest floor. When Dee and I sat down, he hopped over to us. At first I thought he was just curious about us. But then I realized that he was hoping I would help him out!

I decided to push some leaves aside on the forest floor. Right away he went over to the leaves that I had disturbed. On my hands and

SAY THE WORD!

Alpine: high in the mountains, especially above the timberline

Sensitive area: an area that deserves special protection from human development because of its value as habitat for a wide range of plants and animals

Dee and a curious kaka. Kakas have scarlet underwings that you can easily see when they are flying. They are a gorgeous, lowland parrot found only in New Zealand.

knees, I backed up on the trail, pushing leaves as I went. The toutouwai followed me, investigating all the leaves I'd disturbed. I was doing all the work for him. Normally, the toutouwai spends his days on the forest floor, picking up one leaf at a time, tossing it this way and that way, looking for little critters that might be under the leaves.

The toutouwai had no fear of us because it evolved in a place with no predators. The only native mammals on New Zealand are some bats and marine mammals, like seals. Of course, there are some predators on the main islands now!

When humans settled on the islands, they gradually brought possums, birds, cats, dogs, goats, deer, pigs, and sheep. These animals have forever changed New Zealand. Many of these animals, including people, have been slowly decimating the islands' birds.

Kapiti, though, has remained quite untouched by introduced species. There are even kiwis still living on the island of Kapiti. And kiwi birds are rare indeed, seeming almost to be a cross between a mammal and a bird with hair-like feathers and cat-like whiskers. They are also slow and flightless—easy prey. Even though we knew they were there on Kapiti, we never did see a kiwi because we had to leave the island at 4:30 PM. Nobody is allowed to stay overnight. Kiwis are nocturnal birds, and we would have had to spend the night on the island to see one.

After we left Kapiti, Dee and I went to New Zealand's South Island, where we saw the kaka's alpine cousin, the crazy kea! We saw this curious bird when we were on a 4-day hike on Arthur's Pass. On the first night, we camped near a hiker's hostel on the pass. In the morning, I stretched and opened my eyes.

The first thing I saw was the shape of my hiking boots sitting outside through the thin nylon walls of the tent. Then I heard a noise: huffa-huffa-huffa-fook. A bird had flown in and landed right beside the tent. It was a kea, the world's only alpine parrot. He looked around like he was checking to see that the coast was clear. Then, dunka-dunka-dunka-dunk, he hopped closer to the tent. With each hop, his body seemed to grow bigger until he looked like a turkey. I slowly realized that he was about to bend over and grab my hiking boot!

Ziiiiiiip. I unzipped the tent in a flash and the kea stopped and

The red-billed gull is native to New Zealand. It's a typical gull—an aggressive scavenger, despite its small size!

BRIAN'S NOTES

To survive in the harsh mountains, keas have become inquisitive as well as nomadic. This means they'll investigate everything in their path, then travel along to investigate more things so they can use all the food sources they find. Their strong beaks help them pull apart everything from plants and insects to hiking boots.

Our hiking adventures on the Copeland Pass in New Zealand led us over this swinging bridge near a hiker's cabin. The next day, we ascended high into the alpine.

Dee and I hiked the Routeburn Track in New Zealand, and we camped at this stunning site, overlooking the mountains.

looked. Then he turned around and beat it. I rescued the boots. And that was the beginning of all of our experiences with keas.

Another time, we were climbing a big mountain called Avalanche Peak. On the summit, I saw a kea against the beautiful backdrop of the Southern Alps of New Zealand. I pulled off my pack, grabbed my camera, and started taking pictures. Dee did the same. The kea seemed to be posing!

All of a sudden I heard Dee yell, "My pack!" When I turned around to look, I saw Dee's pack catapulting off the mountain. Finally, it lodged about 91 meters (300 ft.) down, in a narrow gully. On the way down, all of Dee's things had fallen out. Well, the kea had a great time. He took off and started helping himself to all the interesting stuff that was scattered down below.

Just as I'd rescued my hiking boots, I started climbing down the mountain to rescue Dee's things. I eventually put everything back in the pack, and you know what, only two of our eggs were broken!

New Zealand is a place Dee and I will never forget. Its curious birds, the kakas, keas, and toutouwais, were just some of the highlights of our trip to the islands of the South Pacific Ocean.

The weka is a large, brown, flightless bird that was traditionally used as food by the Maori people and European settlers. It now faces extinction in many parts of New Zealand.

THE SINGING LEMURS OF THE CLOUD FOREST

Madagascar is about 400 kilometers (249 mi.) off the coast of Mozambique. Even though it's the fourth largest island on Earth, it's a place few outsiders visit. The island's "cloud forests" contain some of the richest plants and trees that Dee and I have ever seen. A cloud forest is a type of rain forest that traps moisture. Every morning we camped in the forest we woke up to a strange rain, even though the sky above the treetops was clear and blue. This was only a hint of the curious things to come on this out-of-the-way island.

Madagascar was formed when it was ripped away from the continent of Africa by plate tectonic action. Then, about 40 million years ago, a large raft of vegetation— probably made from roots and mats of soil torn from a riverbank during a storm— floated to the island from mainland Africa. Against all odds, this raft contained a cargo of lemurs, which would evolve on the isolated island in unimaginable ways.

What is so incredible about the life raft is that it must have carried enough of the lemurs to create a healthy population. Most of the animals that drifted or landed on the Galapagos Islands, for instance, were doomed because they came without mates to have babies. So when enough of a population makes a strange voyage like this, it's quite an accomplishment indeed!

We know that there must have been a life raft because we know that Madagascar split off

Dwarf lemurs, like this one, are the smallest lemurs. You could easily place one in a tea-cup with room to spare!

Just because they have many legs doesn't mean they're fast! In fact, millipedes are quite slow, so they can't outrun predators. Millipedes defend themselves by rolling up, protecting their soft legs inside their armored body parts.

from the rest of Africa *long before* monkeys and lemurs evolved, about 200 million years ago. On the continent of Africa, lemurs were not as successful as they were on the island of Madagascar. On the island, the lemurs had found a safe place with few natural predators—and no competition from the monkeys!

BRIAN'S NOTES

In Malagasy, the language spoken on Madagascar, indri means "Look!" or "There it is!"

Back on the African continent, monkeys evolved alongside their lemur cousins. As the monkeys evolved, they competed with the lemurs for food and territory, and they had faster, stronger bodies and bigger brains to do it. Today only a few types of lemur-like species survive on the continent. These mainland "lemurs" are called galagos and lorises, and all of them have been forced into a nocturnal existence. African monkeys, on the other hand, have evolved into many successful species, but none of them are nocturnal!

Some have teeth that they use to break open bamboo shoots and eat the pith inside. Others are adapted for eating leaves that are far too poisonous for other animals. There are even lemurs that are adapted for eating sap. These lemurs use funny little teeth on their bottom jaw that stick out like buck teeth to break the bark on plants causing the sap to ooze.

While we were on Madagascar, Dee, our guide, and I also tracked down the indri lemur. The indri is Madagascar's most unique lemur, I think. Instead of belching or screaming like all the other lemurs, the indri sings to make itself heard. Its little face turns

The rarely seen aye-aye is a lemur that crawls around in the forest at night and uses its huge, very thin, cat-like ears to listen for the sound of grubs under the bark. When it hears its prey, it pierces the bark like a woodpecker and grabs the grub with a long, tapered middle finger. These are some bark chips left behind by an aye-aye.

On Madagascar there is nary a monkey to be seen because monkeys never got on the raft! In terms of evolution, we can look at the whole island of Madagascar as a kind of life raft for lemurs. Lemurs were free to evolve into every available habitat. New lemurs are being discovered all the time on Madagascar. At least 10 species have been discovered in the last decade alone.

Dee and I were able to see many of these amazing lemurs when we were there. They are ingeniously adapted to their surroundings.

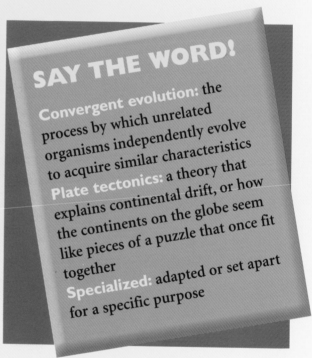

SAY THE WORD!

Convergent evolution: the process by which unrelated organisms independently evolve to acquire similar characteristics

Plate tectonics: a theory that explains continental drift, or how the continents on the globe seem like pieces of a puzzle that once fit together

Specialized: adapted or set apart for a specific purpose

into a trumpet, with its lips pointing outward, and it does this wonderful howl.

Like many lemurs, indris have long, frog-like back legs to help them catapult backwards through the forest canopy. The way an indri moves is called vertical clinging and leaping. You could compare an indri in the forest to a pinball in a pinball game. If I could move in a forest like

Poisonous Frogs

There are more than 450 species of frogs in Madagascar. We found one that is similar to the poisonous dart frogs of South America. It's called the mantella frog. This frog has very poisonous skin. The poison from one frog is enough to wipe out a schoolroom of kids! Like its South American cousins, it is brightly colored to warn other creatures about how poisonous it is. This frog and the poisonous dart frogs in South America are an example of "convergent evolution," where two species have evolved separately but in the same way.

moon, and Dee and I were feeling kind of sad because we were heading home the next day. But then, the indris started to sing all around us. It felt like a special send-off, just for us. Normally indris are daytime lemurs—they don't usually howl at night.

a lemur does, I could get through the canopy of a forest in seconds! Indris turn 180 degrees in mid-air after they catapult from a tree. Then they land on the next tree and start over again. Sometimes the indris hardly even land. They just use that next tree to launch themselves off to another tree. So you see them bouncing through the forest like a pinball. It's outrageous!

I'll never forget camping in our tent, on our last night on Madagascar. It was about two o'clock in the morning, there was a full

We found this odd giraffe-necked weevil, a type of beetle, in Ranomafana National Park.

DANCING IN THE LEK WITH BIRDS OF PARADISE

Papua New Guinea is a place I have wanted to visit since I was 12 years old and started birdwatching. I've always wanted to see the bird of paradise. Actually, there isn't just one bird of paradise. In fact, there are about 42 different kinds and 36 of them are native to New Guinea.

The birds of paradise have evolved in isolation in New Guinea's tropical forests over thousands of years. Each type of bird is adapted to live in the different strata, or layers, of the forest. But most of the birds share two characteristics: The males have the most amazing plumage, and they love to dance!

To show off their plumage and attract females, male birds dance in a display area called a lek. Each species of bird hands down its lek location from one generation to the next. The male birds vie with each other to be the best dancer in the lek. How many females

they mate with depends on how good their dancing is and where in the lek they dance. Would you believe that more than 80 per cent of the female birds mate with one male in the lek? What a dancer!

With most of the females mating with one male, there are some pretty interesting evolutionary results. A dominant trait in the popular male, such as longer tail feathers or an interesting-shaped wattle, will be passed

A highland dancer in Papua New Guinea. With elaborate face paints, amazing wigs, decorative costumes, and headdresses made from the feathers of birds of paradise, New Guinea's highland people have an incredibly colorful culture.

The Hercules moth is one of the largest in the world. Females die after laying their eggs: they have no mouth parts, so they cannot eat! This one is sitting on my hand, almost obscuring it!

This male lesser bird of paradise is displaying his plumage. Lesser birds of paradise will often display in the top branches of "display trees," perfect places to show off their fantastic feathers.

There aren't many mammals in New Guinea, but going there isn't just a bird of paradise safari, either. Going to New Guinea is also a cultural safari. It's a chance to learn about the people who live there.

When Dee and I went to New Guinea, we first went into the highlands. We landed on a

down to most of the chicks he fathers. BANG! The look of a whole generation of birds can change just like that. And there's also a good chance that one of the male chicks is going to grow up to be a popular dancer, too. So the trait is carried on. Perhaps this is why birds of paradise have evolved into such interesting and different types of birds in such a short period of time.

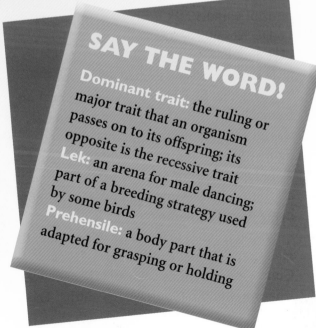

SAY THE WORD!

Dominant trait: the ruling or major trait that an organism passes on to its offspring; its opposite is the recessive trait

Lek: an arena for male dancing; part of a breeding strategy used by some birds

Prehensile: a body part that is adapted for grasping or holding

Here I am with some children, figuring out the bird of paradise feathers on their fathers' headdresses. Sometimes we found birds of paradise right in the villages. The people harvested birds for traditional reasons, but they weren't destroying the population.

tiny runway near Mount Hagen, and then we drove to Ambua Lodge in the rain forest not far away. At the lodge, we met our guide, Joseph Tano. He knew very little English, but he was one of the best birdwatchers in the land. People who want to make films about birds of paradise ask for Joseph of Ambua Lodge. Now, this is the kind of guy I really like!

Joseph was always excited about any birdsong that he heard. If he heard a birdsong from a bird that we hadn't seen yet, then it was an all-out effort to find that bird and figure out what it was. Without Joseph, it would have been impossible for me to find any birds in New Guinea on my own without being there for months.

Joseph belongs to a remarkable culture, the Huli Clan. The highland people of New Guinea are incredibly colorful. The men wear what we would call outrageous outfits. They have huge headdresses, gourd clothing, beaded clothing, and different kinds of face paints applied in certain ways. The men also wear big wigs made out of human hair during ceremonies.

Dee and I were invited to a village to observe a ceremonial dance. The men wore bright paints, their great headdresses, and these gourds instead of pants. The thing that struck me about the dancing was how bird-like it was. It was almost as if the men had learned a thing or two from the birds of paradise in their leks—not just the way they danced but also the way they dressed up. Most of the headdresses in the New Guinea highlands are made from bird of paradise feathers.

Even though I don't speak any of the many languages spoken in New Guinea, I found a way highlands, such as the bizarre tree kangaroo. Tree kangaroos started out as a species living in trees, then they evolved to take advantage of grass. But something odd happened. One of them was hopping around on the grass and looked up into the trees and said, "Hmm … leaves." Tree kangaroos evolved *backwards*, back up into the trees—and there they stayed.

The tree kangaroo has a special ankle joint so it can walk along a tree branch. It also has a prehensile tail, a tail that can grasp things. Just like other leaf-eaters, such as koalas and pandas, tree kangaroos have to sleep for about 85 per cent of the day. Leaves are full of poisons and are difficult to digest, so leaf-eaters spend a lot of their time sleeping to digest them.

Dee and I had an amazing time in New Guinea, both in the highlands and in the low-lands, meeting the people and finally seeing the birds of our dreams.

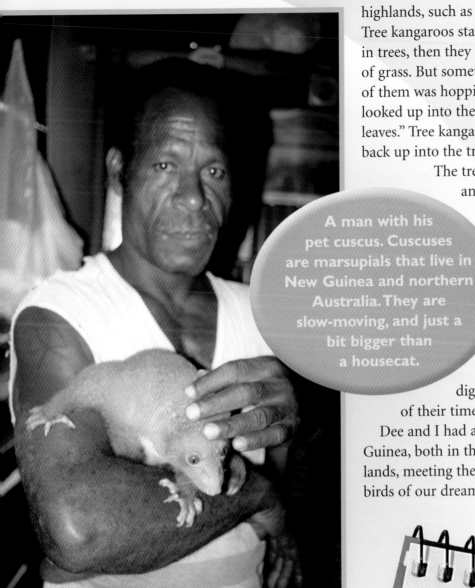

A man with his pet cuscus. Cuscuses are marsupials that live in New Guinea and northern Australia. They are slow-moving, and just a bit bigger than a housecat.

to get along with the people we met. I pulled out my bird book and opened it up to the birds of paradise page, showed it to some children, and right away one of them would run off and get his dad's headdress. After that, it was a headdress show-and-tell free-for-all! We would sit there with the kids and try to figure out which feathers on the headdress belonged to which species of bird of paradise.

We saw other animals in the New Guinea

BRIAN'S NOTES

There are about 800 languages spoken in New Guinea, and just as many different cultures. This is probably because of the rough terrain and lack of roads that separate the isolated populations of people.

THE CRAZY CICHLIDS OF LAKE MALAWI

Malawi is a country on the east side of Africa. The main feature of the country is a long, deep lake called Lake Malawi. This lake is famous because of its cichlid fish. Because the lake is remote and hasn't changed for a long time, the freshwater cichlids have become like the lemurs of Madagascar. They have exploded into a variety of different and interesting species.

Lake Malawi itself is an "island" of water surrounded by people and agriculture. Here's this body of water that has been untouched for millions of years. The only things that have affected it are floods and droughts, which have caused the lake waters to rise and fall countless times over the years.

Scientists think that lake levels have forced the cichlid fish to diversify, or adapt and change. They have to search for new niches in a smaller, more competitive environment when the amount of water in the lake falls. When the lake fills up again, the individual fish populations have

Lake Malawi National Park, on the southern end of the lake, is a World Heritage site. By studying the fish diversity, evolutionary biologists can gain a better understanding of how creatures adapt to survive in a changing environment.

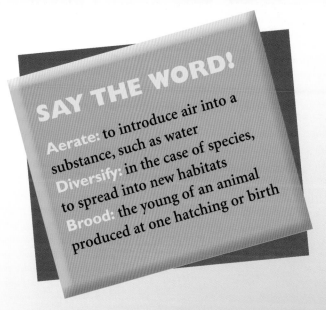

SAY THE WORD!

Aerate: to introduce air into a substance, such as water

Diversify: in the case of species, to spread into new habitats

Brood: the young of an animal produced at one hatching or birth

log. The canoes have pointed ends and are hollowed out just enough for the fishermen's legs to fit in the canoe, while they sit on top of the log. These canoes may seem hard to balance, but they're not if you've grown up paddling the lake, fishing Lake Malawi for cichlids.

You can tell cichlids apart by their color, the shapes of their mouths, where they live, and what they eat.

Cichlids have 2 set of jaws: I in the mouth to suck, scrape, or bite off food; the other in the throat to crush, slice, and pierce the food before swallowing.

changed so much that some become new and different species.

Dee and I were keen to go snorkeling and scuba diving and to meet the people who live in Malawi. We found out about a kayaking company that allows you to kayak to a couple of different islands on the lake.

The fishermen who paddle the lake use dugout canoes that they have carved from a single

As we kayaked on the lake, we would sometimes pass close enough to the fishermen to wave to them and talk to them. We couldn't speak their language, but they understood that we wanted to take pictures of their fish. I was able to look at the many different types of cichlids that they were catching, one at a time. This cichlid, part of a fisherman's catch, has a baby fish poking out of its mouth.

On the island of Domwe there was a huge baobab tree. A ladder was set up beside the tree with a sign that read: "Climb up this ladder at your own risk, please keep in mind that the nearest medical services are many days' travel away." I managed to climb way up into the top of this tree. While I was up there, I watched some weaver finches working on their nests. I also had a great view of the lake and all the fishermen on it.

But there are basically two different kinds of these fish. There are the colorful ones and the not-so-colorful ones. The colorful cichlids live in the rocky areas, while the dull ones live in the sandy areas. They've all evolved in different ways to get their food. The most interesting fact for me is that all cichlids are mouth brooders.

Cichlids swallow their youngsters to keep them safe. Dee and I would snorkel over the feeding areas of the colorful cichlids. We would find a beautiful little garden of green algae on a rock the size of a kitchen table. Several fish would be hanging out in the garden, eating the algae. Then, suddenly, we would notice one cichlid clearing all the other fish away from the garden. It would then move to the middle of the garden and spit out all of its youngsters.

All of these babies would come out—POOF—like a little cloud. I counted one mouthful of at least 40 little babies. They would stay close together around their mother, feeding on algae, counting on her to protect them from the predator cichlids. These predators would scream in at lightning speed and try to pick off the babies.

Here I am snorkeling in Lake Malawi. Dee and I spent a great deal of time floating on the top of the lake's waters, watching cichlids.

If a mother saw a predatory cichlid come in to her feeding area, she called her babies in and gulped them up. She usually needed a few gulps to bring all of the babies in safe and sound. I watched one mother successfully bring almost all 40 of her babies into her mouth, even as she tried to chase other predators away. One baby was stolen at the very end.

It was sad, and it explained why some of the females I saw spewed out only 6 or 7 babies in the algae gardens. Losing 1 baby per feeding can be costly.

After we left the rock areas, we would snorkel over the sandy areas of the lake. The sandy areas have more dull-looking cichlids. The duller colors help camouflage, or hide, the fish. We came across a huge crater, about 1 meter (3 ft.) across, carved out by a cichlid. This was a nest.

A "sandy" male cichlid will prove how amazing he is to females by building a huge nesting site called a "bower." He will pick up a couple of sand grains at a time and create raised doughnut shapes, which he defends vigorously. The bigger the doughnut nest, the

Cichlids are unique among fish because they invest a lot of time and energy into their broods. They lay as few as 10 eggs, and watch over them so they survive.

more attractive the male is to females. After all, if he has all that energy and ability to build a nest and defend it, then he must be a good catch!

When the female chooses her male, she mates with him, lays her eggs in the nesting area, and immediately picks up the eggs. He makes sure that the eggs are fertilized before the female leaves his bower. The male is ready to receive other females into his bower. The

female must now incubate the eggs for about three weeks inside her mouth. By inhaling fresh water, she aerates the eggs to make sure there's a current flowing over them all the time so they have oxygen. When they hatch, the female continues to carry the tiny babies in her mouth. She only releases them when they are able to swim.

Another type of cichlid we found is called a fin eater. We observed these creative feeders in the "sandy" habitat, watching them explode up from the lake bed to catch other fish and snip off their fins. They take a mouthful each time. So you see cichlids swimming around all over the place with tattered fins.

The variety of bizarre cichlids is amazing. One looks like a floating, dead cichlid. It even has light-colored patches that look like rotting flesh. When other cichlids come up to feed on it, it pounces.

Lake Malawi has escaped the ravages of introduced species. Other lakes in the world have lost their native fish to bigger, faster fish that people have introduced. Still, the cichlids are amazing fish that need to be protected. What an experience to kayak around Lake Malawi, visiting its islands and the unique fish that live in its waters.

One group of cichlids is called "thick lipped." They seal their lips around rock openings and suck crustaceans out of cracks and rocks. Certain types of thick lips have evolved to suck creatures out of specifically shaped cracks. These thick-lipped cichlids look like they have been in too many fist fights!

BRIAN'S NOTES

There are about 850 known species of cichlids in Lake Malawi. I think there will be many more discovered soon since the fish living in the deeper parts of the lake have hardly been noted yet.

Dee photographed this pair of fish eagles right outside the front door of our tent. Fish eagles are specialized fish-eating birds of prey, catching their food feet-first!

MURRELETS ON HAIDA GWAII

The Queen Charlotte Islands (Haida Gwaii) is an archipelago, or group, of 138 islands, in western Canada's waters. I think they are one of the most exciting places I've been to in Canada.

One amazing thing about Haida Gwaii is the temperate, old-growth rainforests there. These rainforests were nearly all cut down not very long ago. But in the 1970s, the Haida people and environmentalists stood up for them, and we've been realizing their importance ever since. These giant trees cradle the most amazing life forms, from low-lying mushrooms to high-flying birds.

Because the islands are remote and safe from predators, many birds, such as the ancient murrelet, nest there. The murrelets and other sea birds fly in at night to avoid the peregrine falcons and other predators that might be around. The story of the ancient murrelets is a story of survival against all odds.

Dee and I joined a group of biologists to find out more about these ancient murrelets. One night, we put our tarp down on the thick green moss and put our sleeping bags on the tarp and waited for the murrelets to arrive. Several hours after darkness descended upon the forest, we suddenly heard this "chhchcchch-a-doodoo doo"—the sound of rapid little wings flying through the forest.

Walking along in the forest on Haida Gwaii, you might hear the beautiful, crystal-clear call of the winter wren chatting. There is also often the flute-like call of the 2 or 3 species of thrush, such as this Swainson's thrush.

The temperate old-growth forests of Haida Gwaii are Canadian treasures, supporting a variety of species. The trees are so big and the moss is so deep that we felt like little gnomes walking through the forest.

Then the murrelets started hitting the tree branches and tumbling down onto the ground. They were like snowballs pummeling all around us. Sometimes the birds landed right beside us, and then they scurried like rats all around, trying to find the holes that they'd created in the moss. They had arrived to bring their babies out to sea.

When the parent murrelets call for their youngsters at the entrance to the nest, the chicks come out. As the chicks emerge, the parents fly off to the ocean. From beyond the breakers, they continually call. Even though the night is alive with the calls of other adult murrelets, the youngsters know their parents' voices.

SAY THE WORD!

Mortuary: related to burial practices

Smallpox: a deadly and disfiguring disease unique to humans

Temperate rainforest: coniferous or broadleaf forests that occur between the tropics and the polar regions in areas of high rainfall

Each ancient murrelet egg weighs about one quarter the weight of the mother bird! That's like a 46-kg (100-lb.) human giving birth to an 11-kg (25-lb.) baby. Ouch! Murrelet chicks are able to walk within 24 hours of hatching.

The bouncy little chicks were like popcorn bursting out of a hot pan. They had the superhero ability to hop over deadfall logs. Eventually they all ran down to the ocean.

The chicks hopped in the water and spun their little legs, heading toward the open ocean and their parents' voices. Big waves would come in and crash down on the chicks, tossing them back to the beach, but they got up again, shook themselves off, and ran back to the water. Eventually the birds made it over the big waves to meet with their parents.

When they finally reunite with their parents, the birds have to swim non-stop until sunrise so they can get 5 to 15 kilometers (3.1 to 9.3 mi.) out into the open

ocean. They do this to get past the point where bald eagles or peregrine falcons might come and pluck them like grapes off a vine. As soon as they are in open water, they can start making a living and survive. Ancient murrelets are the only seabirds that raise their young entirely at sea!

The only problem with nesting on these remote islands comes when people start messing with things. In the 1940s the Canadian government permitted an introduction of raccoons onto the islands to encourage a fur trade. But in the mild climate of the Queen Charlottes, the raccoons never developed a big fur coat, so they weren't commercially useful.

When the raccoons got to Haida Gwaii, they must have thought, "Holy Cow! No predators?!"

SGang Gwaay

Haida Gwaii was once a place of cultural wonderment. A Haida saying goes, "when the tide goes out, the table is set." Because the Haida people didn't have to work hard for food, they were able to develop a rich cultural life. The Haida also had longhouses in which they stayed during the rainy, dreary winters. It was in these longhouses that the people developed their visual arts, storytelling, and a wonderful sense of humor.

One day, though, Europeans came along and gave the Haida people smallpox. A ship actually kicked a sailor with smallpox off onto Haida Gwaii, knowing that his disease would kill all of the Native people. Sure enough, 90 per cent of all the Haida died. There is one town once called Ninstints, now called SGang Gwaay, where everyone died.

SGang Gwaay is hidden in a little cove, and because no one was left living there, the place was forgotten. When souvenir collectors and museums started taking totem poles from Haida Gwaii, they largely missed SGang Gwaay. You can still paddle in to this amazing place with its tall, beautifully carved mortuary poles, which are like gravestones. It would have been a wonderful place to live, sheltered from storms and enemies within the trees and thick moss. You can almost hear children laughing on the beach. You can almost see the amazing Haida canoes paddling in the water, and hear the sound of wood being chopped for the fire.

SGang Gwaay mortuary poles. Walking through SGang Gwaay was a quieting, spiritual experience.

Exploring the tide pools of Haida Gwaii is a true treat! Finding clusters of anemones, starfish, and sea urchins is not uncommon when the tide goes out.

Every time the tide goes out, tidal pools are full of sea creatures. The variety of colorful starfish, clams, and mussels are all there for the raccoons. And the birds and their nests are there for the raccoons, too.

We went to one island with raccoons, and at every nest site of ancient murrelets we found feathers. It was as if somebody had had a pillow fight and the pillow broke. There were feathers all over the forest floor. How long can a bird species last with that kind of hunting going on? Now there is a team of people on the islands who are trying get rid of the raccoons.

The Queen Charlotte Islands definitely has its challenges, but it's a phenomenal place. I like to visit the islands by ketch, which is a type of sailboat. There's nothing quite as

The Queen Charlotte Basin is home to 5 species of pinnipeds—harbor seals, steller sea lions, California sea lions, elephant seals, and northern fur seals. Only the harbor seals are year-round residents.

Sea urchins are common in the waters of Haida Gwaii, and sea otters eat sea urchins. Although sea otters always did live near Haida Gwaii, they were wiped out years ago by the fur trade. They have not come back in any number to the islands, although some have been seen off SGang Gwaay. These are river otters, which are common on the beach, especially at low tide.

BRIAN'S NOTES

Old-growth forests have never experienced a forest fire. Big trees eventually fall, opening up a little sparkle of light in the middle of the forest, which then allows new growth to start. The old fallen trees are called "nursery trees" because they provide a nutrient base for new trees, bacteria, slugs, you name it.

beautiful as anchoring beside an island in May, which is when all the birds are singing. If you get up about half an hour before sunrise you can see the sea mist, and the water is glassy and calm. There might even be a black bear on the beach, rooting away. It's truly a magical, powerful place.

SEARCHING FOR THE "MAN OF THE FOREST"

There are three great apes on Earth. Dee and I have spent time with Jane Goodall and her chimpanzees in East Africa. We have also been to Rwanda, Uganda, and the Democratic Republic of the Congo in search of mountain gorillas. Lastly, we have seen orangutans on the island of Borneo, the third largest island in the world.

Because of forest fires and people logging the forests in Borneo, the wild orangutans have been quickly disappearing. We thought we should go to Borneo and see them in the wild before it was too late.

We flew into Kuching, the capital city in the state of Sarawak, Malaysia, a country in Borneo. Here we hired a guide by the name of Lemon Praddy Ales—he would help us find orangutans in the jungle.

Lemon, Dee, and I struck out in a jeep and drove all the way into the interior of Borneo to the Sarawak Mountains. At the head of the Batang Ai Reservoir, Lemon, Dee, and I left the

SAY THE WORD!

Brachiation: to move by swinging with the arms from one hold to another

Orangutan: means "man of the forest" in the Malay language

Primary forest: old-growth forest sometimes millions of years old

car behind and got on a longboat to travel up the Laland River. The captain of the boat was a skilled driver, and his helper was a 14-year-old boy who stood at the front and used a pole to direct the boat away from rocks in the shallow waters of the river.

As we made our way past logging areas into the primary forest to find and watch the rare and usually silent orangutan, we had many

Edmund Untam was the bowman on the boat Dee and I rode up the Laland River. He would pull out a little fishnet every now and then, and throw it into a calm part of the water. Sometimes he would catch one or two fish just big enough to fry in the pan at night.

adventures. We stayed in a tourist longhouse at Nanga Sumpa, which was connected to a village longhouse by a bridge. This longhouse was similar to the ones used by the Haida people on the Queen Charlotte Islands (see the previous story for more on them). It was fascinating because we were able to meet the people and catch a glimpse of longhouse culture. Longhouses are amazing. The living room of a longhouse can

The Nanga Sumpa longhouse is located right on the Laland River. The chief invited us into the longhouse for only a short time to minimize the impact of our foreign culture on his people.

be 30 to 40 meters (98 to 131 ft.) long and 8 to 9 meters (26 to 30 ft.) wide. This long room is where all the cooking, ceremonies, and dances happen. Every family in the village has its own private living quarters attached to the living room. The whole longhouse is built on poles above the ground. When it's raining cats and dogs, the village is high and dry.

We slept well at our longhouse, and in the morning we pressed on up the river. The forest canopy above the river enclosed us. It was as if we were going through a green tube with a watery base—kind of like a water slide, but going backwards! We sometimes had to jump out and help the boat over rapids or around sharp corners.

We slept that night in a bark hut. I think that was the hottest night I've ever spent! We were excited about what we would find the next day.

The next morning at sunrise we started hiking the steep slopes into the forest. To find an orangutan in the wild, you must listen for the swish of a branch above your head. It could be the sound of an orangutan

Orangutans live in the trees on Borneo and Sumatra. The orangutan is the biggest arboreal, or tree, ape.

Orangutans never seem to let go of a branch before they've got hold of the next one. If they can't grab a particular branch, they will shake the tree they're on back and forth, like a big hairy pendulum, until they are close enough to grab the branch.

Lemon Praddy Ales, our longboat guide, and me. Lemon would collect the food we would eat at night as we traveled up the river.

macaques who were very surprised to see us, and a barking deer. But no orangutans. We went farther into the forest than Lemon had ever gone. He was marking the trees with his machete so we could find our way out again.

We were disappointed when we started walking back toward our campsite at the end of the day. But then we heard the swish of a branch. Very quietly, with our hearts pounding in our chests, we stopped and looked above us. Through the thick trees Lemon spotted two faces looking at us.

Seeing two orangutans together is unusual. The only times you will see more than one at a time are when a male and female are mating, a female is with her baby, or two brothers are hanging out together. We think we saw the brother combo.

Lemon, Dee, the orangutans, and I looked at each other for about 20 minutes. We just bathed in this first view of one of the most remarkable primates on the planet. Finally, in real Tarzan mode, the brothers swung by their arms, doing a brachiation up through the trees. We could hear the swish of the branches as they left us. At one point we heard a really loud CRACK, so one of them must have broken a branch.

When we left the forest, Lemon confessed to us that he had never caught sight of any orangutans in that spot until that time with Dee and me. He couldn't wait to go back to the office and tell all the others—it was a real badge of honor for him. And it was one of the best 20 minutes I've ever spent, looking into the eyes of wild orangutans in Sarawak. Of course, we also went to Sabah, another state in Malaysia, which you'll read about in the next story.

moving from one tree to the next. We would walk for ten minutes, then stop and listen for five minutes. We knew that the only way to find orangutans was to walk, stop, and listen, because orangutans are very quiet.

After two days of searching, we had found some of the orangutans' tree nests, a troop of

BRIAN'S NOTES

Researchers have found that 7 out of 10 orangutans have broken an arm or leg bone in their lives. Even though they're careful, orangutans sometimes fall out of the trees. It must be painful, and the orangutan would have to wait until the leg or arm healed. But they do heal.

THE LAND OF THE HORNBILL

After Dee and I saw the wild orangutans in the Sarawak Mountains, we decided to visit the state of Sabah, Malaysia, too. Our journey there was like being in a Walt Disney movie. There were laughter, tears, and joy. We went to Sabah to visit a nature reserve in the Danum Valley that is renowned the world over. The Borneo Rainforest Lodge is a wonderful example of a big business giving back to the environment and conserving many animal, plant, and bird species in the process.

Getting to the reserve was the sad part. We saw terrible destruction along the way. To travel from Sarawak to Sabah, you have to go through clear-cut forests. It's a horrible thing to clear-cut huge areas of forest where the topsoil then washes away. Loggers can use something called "selective logging" to cut trees and leave the variety of living things more or less intact. But it is cheaper and easier for some logging companies to go in and take everything.

Clear-cut logging leaves nothing for anybody, especially in wet, tropical rainforests, which have never before seen fires or clear-cut logging. Eventually the forest grows back, but that forest is not the same. There are fewer species of trees and plant life than in the primary forest that was cut down, and the animals are gone forever.

We drove through mud and destruction, passing by logging trucks that had only a few huge logs on them. But then we turned a corner and arrived at the nature reserve. This reserve is a large area of primary forest that the logging company itself has preserved, leaving part of the forest behind for the next generation.

While we were at the Sepilok Orangutan Sanctuary, we had to stay on a boardwalk. The orangutans in this sanctuary are being conditioned to return to the wild.

Wallace's flying frog

BRIAN'S NOTES

Wallace's flying frog is about the size of your fist and has huge toes and huge fingers. Between those toes and fingers is a thin film of skin that acts like a parachute. The frog is named after Alfred Russell Wallace, who worked separately from Charles Darwin toward a theory of the way species evolve on Earth. Wallace also put his name on a part of the world called the Wallace Line. It's an imaginary line that divides the unique animals of Asia from the distinct animals of Australia.

We would be staying at the Rainforest Lodge in the middle of the reserve. The lodge was designed by naturalists to step lightly on the forest floor. The building is built on stilts with wooden walkways. Any plants that were removed when the lodge was being built were replanted to attract butterflies and birds. As soon as I got out of the car and walked toward the lodge, I saw butterflies the size of tea-cup saucers, with long proboscises sucking the nectar of flowers.

The name Sabah means "land of the hornbill," and the hornbill is a big beautiful bird. When we were driving through Sabah to reach the reserve, we didn't see any hornbills at all. But within 48 hours of reaching the Rainforest Lodge, we saw all 7 species of hornbill that are native to Borneo. The reserve gave us a real view into the way the forest must have looked a hundred years ago.

We saw wild jungle fowl, the ancestors of

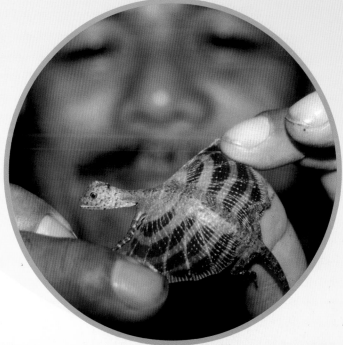

Flying lizards make their homes in Sabah. They have webbed extensions on the end of their ribcages that have evolved into fins, like the fins on a fish. The lizards can stretch those fins out, jump off a tree, and glide to the next tree.

all farm chickens the world over. We saw evidence of the forest elephants—dollops of their dung on the road. And as we were having lunch one day, a Borneo bearded pig snuffled into view.

Borneo bearded pigs are endemic to Borneo. They have a long pig face with whiskers that look like toilet bowl brushes on either side of their nose. In most of Borneo the bearded pig has disappeared, but there it was, like a ghost from the past, in the reserve.

Another creature we saw that is usually impossible to see on Borneo is the banded civet. The civet is one of Borneo's predators. One night we were walking in the forest and we heard a civet. I thought I might be able to call it in closer to us using a technique I've used before to lure in predators. I pursed my lips and made a "squeak squeak squeak" sound. Any carnivore is usually interested in this sound of a mouse in trouble! Almost immediately, the civet came out of the forest.

One morning Dee and I got up at 4 AM and climbed into a tree canopy pathway that was set up on the reserve. These walkways went from one huge tropical tree to the next. We sat 40 meters (131 ft.) above the ground on a platform, right in the canopy of the forest, and listened to the nighttime

By mimicking a mouse in distress I was able to lure in a banded civet. This is a Malagasy civet that I photographed in Madagascar. It looks very similar to the one I saw in Borneo.

sounds of the crickets disappear. The daytime sounds of birds and gibbons slowly drowned out the fading sounds of frogs, crickets, and bats. It was one of the most remarkable mornings of my life.

By 7 AM the forest was quiet. At 7:30, still sitting in the same place, we looked down about 6 meters (20 ft.) and saw a hairy red arm coming out of the tree to grab some fruit and pull it back in. The whole time we were sitting on the platform, a female orangutan had been with us! We sat in the same spot and watched her get out of her nest. Then we watched her move from one branch to another, gathering

SAY THE WORD!

Biodiversity: variety of life on Earth, measured by variety within species and ecosystems

Proboscis: a long, flexible snout

Selective logging: the removal of trees in a stand according to specific guidelines, such as height, circumference, and form

The Sepilok Orangutan Sanctuary

We went to an orangutan sanctuary in Sabah. With all the logging and forest fires in Borneo, orangutans are being forced out of the forests and into farming areas. The adults are usually killed, and the babies stay with the farmers as pets. A baby orangutan is only cute until it grows up and starts ripping up the curtains or biting its owners. The babies end up in sanctuaries, where people try to get them used to the wild again.

The Sepilok sanctuary feeds the orangutans milk and bananas, a boring diet that encourages them to get out into the forest and find their own fruit. When the researchers at the sanctuary think an orangutan is ready to go back to the wild, they catch it and release it. The problem is that there's a diminishing amount of wild forest to return to.

Canopy walks, like the one Dee and I took in Sabah, are amazing, but only if you arrive before dawn. If you get there after 8:00 AM, you miss most of the show. It would be like arriving at a hockey game just as everyone else is leaving.

Male orangutans weigh up to 90 kg (198 lb.), and females up to 50 kg (110 lb.). Because they are so big, they have to be very careful about how they move high up in the trees.

different types of fruit until she disappeared.

Sabah is the least populated part of Borneo with the best tropical rainforest reserve I've ever visited. It just goes to show that even the biggest businesses can give back to the environment if they choose to. When people ask me where they should go when they visit Borneo, I always say Sabah—it's where the forest comes alive.

CONSERVATION—IT'S UP TO YOU

If you'd like to learn more about or become involved in wildlife conservation, contact any or all of the following organizations.

Calgary Zoo
1300 Zoo Road, SE
Calgary, Alberta, Canada T2E 7V6
1-403-232-9333
www.calgaryzoo.ab.ca

Canadian Parks and Wilderness Society
National Office
880 Wellington Street, Suite 506
Ottawa, Ontario, Canada K1R 6K7
info@cpaws.org   1-800-333-WILD
www.cpaws.org

Canadian Nature Federation
1 Nicholas Street, Suite 606
Ottawa, Ontario, Canada K1N 7B7
cnf@cnf.ca   1-613-562-3447
www.cnf.ca

Canadian Wildlife Federation
350 Michael Cowpland Drive
Kanata, Ontario, Canada K2M 2W1
info@cwf-fcf.org   1-800-563-WILD
www.cwf-fcf.org

Charles Darwin Research Station
Puerto Ayora, Santa Cruz
Galapagos Islands, Ecuador
cdrs@fcdarwin.org.ec   (593) 5 2526-146/147

David Suzuki Foundation
2211 West 4th Avenue, Suite 219
Vancouver, British Columbia, Canada V6K 4S2
solutions@davidsuzuki.org   1-800-453-1533
www.davidsuzuki.org

Ducks Unlimited (Wetland Conservation)
Box 1160
Oak Hammock Marsh, Manitoba, Canada R0C 2Z0
1-800-665-3835
www.ducks.ca

Earthwatch International
3 Clock Tower Place, Suite 100
Box 75
Maynard, Massachusetts, USA 01754
1-800-776-0188
www.earthwatch.org

The Jane Goodall Institute (Canada)
Mr. Nicolas Billon, Executive Assistant
P. O. Box 477, Victoria Station
Westmount, Quebec, Canada H3Z 2Y6
nicolas@janegoodall.ca   1-514-369-3384 (fax)
www.janegoodall.ca

Laskeek Bay Conservation Society
PO Box 867
Queen Charlotte, British Columbia, Canada V0T 1S0
info@laskeekbay.org   1-250-559-2345
www.laskeekbay.org

Marmot Recovery Foundation
Marmot
Box 2332, Station A
Nanaimo, British Columbia, Canada V9R 6X9
1-877-4MARMOT
www.marmots.org

Orangutan Foundation International
7 Kent Terrace, London, UK NW1 4RP
info@orangutan.org.uk   +44 (0)20 7724 2912
www.orangutan.org.uk

Cool Sites on the Web:
Charles Darwin Foundation: www.darwinfoundation.org
Gwaii Haanas National Park Reserve:
http://www.pc.gc.ca/pn-np/bc/gwaiihaanas/index_e.asp
Species At Risk: www.speciesatrisk.ca
Space for Species: www.spaceforspecies.ca

INDEX

Cover and interior illustrations by Brian and Dee Keating, except on page 23 (top left) (by Taman Safari, Bogor, Indonesia), pages 26, 27 (middle) (by Alessia Comini), and pages 28–29, 30, 31 (top) (by Ad Konings)
Cover and interior design by John Luckhurst
Edited by Meaghan Craven
Copyedited by Ann Sullivan
Proofread by Lesley Reynolds
Scans by ABL Imaging

The publisher gratefully acknowledges the support of The Canada Council for the Arts and the Department of Canadian Heritage.

THE CANADA COUNCIL | LE CONSEIL DES ARTS
FOR THE ARTS | DU CANADA
SINCE 1957 | DEPUIS 1957

We acknowledge the financial support of the Government of Canada through the Book Publishing Industry Development Program (BPIDP) for our publishing activities.

Printed in China

06 07 08 09 10 / 5 4 3 2 1

First published in the United States in 2006 by
Fitzhenry & Whiteside
311 Washington Street, Brighton,
Massachusetts 02135

National Library of Canada Cataloguing in Publication Data

Keating, Brian, 1955
Amazing animal adventures on islands / with Brian Keating.

Includes index. ISBN 1-894856-58-9 (bound)
ISBN 1-894856-59-7 (pbk.)
ISBN 1-894856-56-2 (Teacher's guide)

1. Island animals—Juvenile literature. I. Title.
QL111K43 2006   j591.752   C2006-902928-8

Fifth House Ltd.
A Fitzhenry & Whiteside Company
1511, 1800-4 St. SW
Calgary, Alberta T2S 2S5

1-800-387-9776
www.fitzhenry.ca

ACKNOWLEDGEMENTS

There are many people who have inspired me in my work as a naturalist.

I would like to thank: Randy Burke, owner of Blue Water Adventures in Vancouver, who captained the ship *Island Roamer* on my first of several voyages to the Queen Charlotte Islands, taking me to some of the best remote coves and inlets; Lemon Ales, who led us deep into the forests of Borneo to find wild orangutans and so much more; Willie and Dorothy Pyle, who fed and sheltered us during the big hurricane in Hawaii that threatened to dampen our spirits; Denell Falk and the wonderful ladies at Civilized Adventures, who flawlessly get us there and back with such enthusiasm; Ad Konings, the world cichlid expert, for his encouragement and photos 'for the cause'; biologist Rob Butler for his advice and guidance on this book project; the Laskeek Conservation Society, which took me in and showed me the hidden secrets of the ancient murrelet; Gwen Wawn at Safari Consultants in Zimbabwe, a good friend and fellow explorer, who put us in touch with Kayak Africa in Malawi, which in turn introduced us to those jewel islands where cichlids entered my life in full, glorious color; and finally, the guides who have taken us to so many islands in so many amazing places, introducing us to the plants, birds, reptiles, and the mammals that live there. All of you have given me such inspiration and insight into what life is all about on the islands of the world. Thank you, too, to the Calgary Zoo, for enabling my childhood dreams of exploring the world's wild areas, including islands, to come true. And thanks to the people who have come on "ZooFari" trips with me: you have been wonderful traveling companions.

And most important, I would like to thank my wife Dee, who shares my love for exploring islands and who is my dedicated travel partner.

DON'T FORGET!

Amazing Animal Adventures Around the World
Amazing Animal Adventures at the Poles
Amazing Animal Adventures in the Desert
Amazing Animal Adventures in Rivers